How To Manage Your Money

In This Straightforward Guide To Personal Finance, You Will Learn How To Save Money, Invest It, Pay Taxes, Create A Budget, And Avoid Falling Victim To Financial Scams

Edmund Campbell

TABLE OF CONTENT

You Are Not Employed By The Money...1

Financial Source You Use Is Fluid 5

Identify A Coach And A Mentor...22

Advice For An Ideal Financial Life Free From Crisis........39

Act Honourable 85

Manage Your Money And Ensure It Produces More Earnings For You. 114

Speak With Your Debtors 141

YOU ARE NOT EMPLOYED BY THE MONEY

There aren't many people seated at this table, but you might be the only one. Over the years, I've observed that people's lack of self-employment contributes to their careless spending. Though it might come as a surprise, it is really accurate. It's time to reconsider your spending if it's the cause of your current habits.

The freebie mentality operates in this way: since you don't have to work hard to obtain what you have, you tend to abuse it. This is terrible because, should you be given the opportunity, you might easily spend all of the money in a bank without exerting any effort. Freebies don't always bring out the best in people. It's stated that you will understand the worth of every drop of water if you carry your bucket.

The harsh reality is that freebies are no longer valuable. In other words, it doesn't persist for very long. At some time, whoever is giving you free money will cease and demand that you take care of yourself. If a farmer consumes all of his produce, he will never have enough seeds for the following planting season. Act like no farmer at all!

Remember this always: nobody enjoys being a liability. Over-reliance on other people turns you into one. While the sun is shining, make hay!

Fifth: You're feeding your addiction

Being an addict is one of the easiest ways to spend money carelessly. You did really hear correctly. One of the simplest ways to squander money without exerting any thought or sweat is through addiction. Addiction can be defined as a person's intense attachment to something or a behaviour that seems out of control. Addiction has a stronger hold. This is where the servicing comes in, and the majority of addicts require financial servicing.

Addiction manifests itself in a multitude of ways, including smoking, sex, food, materialism, pornography, and movies. Anything you find difficult to stop doing and that you find yourself reverting to helplessly is a sign that you are hooked to it. You may be feeding your addiction, which could be one of the reasons you spend the way you do.

You might wonder how watching films on my computer or phone ends up costing me extra money. To put it simply, all movie downloads and streams depend on data services, which are paid for with money. Therefore, if you ever discover that you are receiving more data services than you anticipated in a given month, it may be a sign of an addiction that you are unintentionally or knowingly feeding (i.e., what you are doing with the data you are obtaining).

Don't get me wrong, downloading and streaming movies isn't always a terrible thing, but it becomes problematic when it gets to the point where it starts to feel uncomfortable for your pocket. When you're feeding any kind of addiction, it's difficult to maintain finances. The issue with feeding an addiction is that, in order to feed the craving, you have to find a way to borrow money or purchase the item on credit, even if you don't appear to have any. To effectively manage your finances, you need to be aware of and combat your addiction(s).

FINANCIAL SOURCE YOU USE IS FLUID

Here, there's no need to mince words. The likelihood of you spending carelessly is 99% when your source of money is unstable. The way it works is that you develop a mindset that your income is flexible and that other opportunities will present themselves before the current one ends. You can scarcely keep money after your mentality has been formed in this way. Of course, if more money is about to come in, why would you keep it? That is a limited way of thinking.

Nobody is guaranteed tomorrow. Therefore, you have to make do with what you have instead of what will come. That implies that your supply could be cut off at any point rather than that your life would be snatched from you.

An interesting fact about ants is that they gather food in the summer, knowing full well that winter will arrive. They gather as much as they can in the summer, knowing that the winter will not be kind to them. That way, when winter arrives, they'll be safe.

Because your source is erratic, you live for the moment when you spend everything you have. The wise have observed that it is best to strike iron while it is still hot since cold iron cannot be formed into much of any shape. This is the nature of a flexible source of income; if you don't make the most of it while it's coming in, you won't have much left over.

Remember that when a stream's supply is taken off, it dries out. Make the most of your income's flexibility for your gain. Every penny counts!

A few case examples that demonstrate the rat race are as follows:

The Story of Sarah: Sarah, a 35-year-old marketing executive, is employed by a major company. Despite her six-figure income, she is perpetually anxious and worn out due to her demanding work schedule and long hours. She rarely has time or energy for other interests or hobbies because she spends most of her free time shopping and interacting with her coworkers. Sarah makes a lot of money, but because she is stuck in a loop of living paycheck to paycheck and attempting to maintain a certain lifestyle, she is unable to save much or invest in her future. Although she knows she is caught in the never-ending cycle of work and social pressure, she still feels imprisoned by her career.

Mark's Account: Mark, an accountant, has been employed by the same company for more than 20 years. He is 45 years old. Despite having a decent salary and good benefits, he finds his employment to be boring and unfulfilling. Fearful of taking a chance and leaving his secure employment, he longs to launch his own company or pursue a more creative career. Mark has a limited social life outside of work and spends most of his leisure time on the Internet and watching TV. He knows he's in the rat race, but he doesn't feel like he can get out of it.

Lisa's Story: A 28-year-old educator, Lisa is committed to changing her pupils' lives through education. Despite her love for her work, she finds it difficult to live on her meagre pay. She feels that she is always on the verge of financial instability, even though she spends most of her free time tutoring and taking on side jobs to supplement her income. Although Lisa is aware that she is trapped in the rat race, she doesn't think she has many opportunities to earn more money or follow her interests outside of work.

These case studies highlight the various ways in which individuals can get caught up in the never-ending pursuit of wealth, including high-pressure occupations, a fear of failing, and low-wage employment with no opportunity for advancement. These people can start taking action to escape the rat race and pursue a more autonomous and satisfying existence by identifying the patterns and behaviours that keep them locked.

A proactive and deliberate strategy is needed to escape the rat race. To attain financial freedom and build a more satisfying life, we must take this important step, which may not always be simple and may include taking chances and moving outside of our comfort zones.

Detailed guide for establishing financial objectives and formulating a plan of action to reach them

Following the establishment of your budget, evaluation of your financial status, and definition of your financial goals, you should also:

Set priorities for your objectives: Establish the financial objectives that are most essential to you and rank them in order of significance and urgency. This will enable you to concentrate your energies and resources on accomplishing your top priorities first.

Create a strategy to reach your objectives: Create a plan to accomplish each of your financial goals after you've determined which ones are most important. This could entail investing in a diverse portfolio, making a strategy to pay off debt, or establishing precise savings goals. Divide your objectives into more doable, smaller tasks that you can complete every three or four months.

Track your development: Keep a close eye on your progress towards your financial objectives and revise your plan as necessary. This will assist you in staying on course and adjusting your savings, investing, or budget as needed.

Honour your accomplishments: Finally, acknowledge and appreciate your progress. It takes time and dedication to reach financial goals. Therefore, it's critical to recognise your accomplishments and give yourself a treat for your efforts.

The actions above can assist you in setting and completing time-bound, realistic, quantifiable, and specified financial goals, as well as in creating a plan of action to reach them. If you can maintain discipline, focus, and motivation throughout the process, you should have no trouble reaching financial success.

What Is Personal Finance, in Your Opinion?

The planning and administration of one's financial activities, including income generating, spending, saving, investing, and security, is known as personal finance. A budget or financial plan can provide an overview of the personal money management process. This chapter examines the most prevalent and significant facets of personal financial management.

Personal Finance Topics

To fully grasp the subject, we will focus on dissecting the essential components of personal finance in this chapter and going into further detail about each one.

The primary facets of personal finance are income, expenses, savings, and security, as will be discussed below. We'll go into more detail about each of these elements below.

Revenue

An individual's income is the source of cash flow that they receive and utilise to sustain themselves and their family. This marks the beginning of our financial planning phase.

The following are typical sources of income: pensions, wages, dividends, bonuses, and salaries.

A person can spend, save, or invest the money they get from any of these sources of income. In this context, revenue can be viewed as the starting point of our personal finance road plan.

Spending

All personal expenses made in relation to the acquisition or sale of goods and services are considered expenditures (i.e., not investments). Every expense falls into two categories: credit (payable for borrowed money) and cash (payable for cash on hand). The majority of citizens spend the majority of their wealth.

Rent, taxes, food, credit card payments, mortgage payments, entertainment, and travel are common sources of expenditure. These costs take away from an individual's ability to save and invest money. A person has a deficit if their expenses are more than their income. People typically keep an eye on their discretionary spending rather than their profits, despite the fact that managing spending is just as important as generating income. Maintaining sound spending practices is essential to handling personal finances well.

Savings is the process of setting aside extra money for future purchases or investments. A person may choose to save or invest any extra revenue that arises from their expenditures over their income. One important area of personal finance is savings management.

Typical deposits consist of • Hard currency.

- Bank account for savings
- Bank account for checking

Keeping investments helps most people manage their cash flow and the short-term difference between their income and expenses. However, an excessive amount of savings could be considered insufficient as it yields minimal to no returns on investments.

Making Investments

Investing entails buying things that are meant to yield a profit with the hope that the investor will eventually make more money than they first invested. Risks are associated with investing, and not all investments yield a profit. This is where the correlation between risk and return is observed.

Typical investing options include stocks, art, mutual funds, real estate, and commodities.

The most complex component of personal finance is investing, which is also one of the areas where the best guidance is provided. There are big differences in risk and return between different investments, so many people are looking for help with this aspect of their financial strategy.

Defence

A variety of products are needed for personal protection in order to guard against unintentional and dangerous situations.

Typical forms of personal protection include health insurance, life insurance, and estate preparation.

This is another difficult area of personal finance where consumers typically seek professional advice. To precisely ascertain an individual's insurance and estate planning requirements, a comprehensive suite of analyses is required.

phases of personal finance management

Following a well-thought-out plan is essential to proper financial management. A budget or a planned financial plan might incorporate all of the aforementioned personal finance areas.

Typically, personal bankers and investment advisors create these plans after working with their clients to identify their goals and needs and then taking the necessary action.

IDENTIFY A COACH AND A MENTOR

A tutor is somebody with greater experience in business, or simply in daily life, who can assist a visionary in business in honing their skills and encourage them to take on new challenges.

A business coach can be a lifesaver in a variety of scenarios, whether they offer advice on business practices, assist with system administration initiatives. In any case, the most important thing to remember while looking for a tutor is what you want from the programme.

A mentor could be to your mind what a fitness instructor is to your body. By all accounts, using a mentor appears to be the newest strategy for a select few individuals to succeed in today's hectic corporate world.

Profit From Other People

How can the tutor assist you? Finding out what kind of asset you need is a fundamental first step in the guided quest.

A rundown is a good way to introduce yourself. You may need someone with a great audience, social connections, and expertise in supporting open communication. Ideally, you will find a tutor that embodies these qualities, but in reality, you might have to make a few concessions. Once you've determined how many characters you need from a guide, divide that list into many needs.

The next step is to "conduct educational workshops with multiple rivals and then go back to your core values so that you don't lose focus and remain committed to your enterprise or, conversely, local justifications for hiring a tutor." An outstanding competitor will approach you by choosing a combination of the subjective and quantitative qualities of each of your potential mentors.

Recall that having more than one mentor may prove to be advantageous. If you think you might take up too much of your tutor's time, then getting a few manuals might be the best course of action. One benefit of having multiple tutors is that you can participate in group discussions. Additionally, if multiple tutors are present at the same time and are seated around a table, the collaborative energy amongst them actually advances your theory.

Detailed instructions for locating a guide:

Begin with your loved ones, friends, and companions. Start your search for a tutor close to home. Genuinely close and dear. You can occasionally sit down and ask yourself, "Well, what do you feel about this?" to members of your own family or friends—people you know, trust, and can have a conversation with.

Consider the people in your expanded network. If you attempt not to accept that this is the path for you despite receiving enough unwelcome advice from friends, family, and companions, the only people left to choose from are those who either don't know you at all or don't realise you are.

How would you ask a virtual stranger to assume a particularly large responsibility? Reaching out to your network of contacts is the first step.

A complimentary comment from a regular coworker could go a long way towards making a coaching connection seem amazing thus far. Additionally, you should wait to choose a coach until later. This means that you should always have your network ready to meet potential mentors at events like social gatherings and exhibits. Meeting a potential mentor in person fosters a similarity, so you might want to wait until that affiliation makes before making the request.

Look at extreme outcasts: maybe no one in your circle of acquaintances has the makings of a perfect match for you. Start by conducting some research.

Business person profiles in periodicals and newspapers could introduce you to someone who fits your aesthetic. But proceed with caution when you have a few possible outcomes. Learn as much as you can about the potential coach and attempt to arrange a brief phone meeting in which you state that you have no specific needs, only a general interest in learning more about them. You should go to them and, especially at the start, indicate that you would appreciate their assistance as much as possible. After your initial meeting, if everything seems to have gone well, you could suggest that you speak with each other again in the near future, either face-to-face or over the phone. If they continue to respond over time, you may increase the likelihood of a more traditional teaching partnership with clearer goals and boundaries.

Think about the opposition—that is, not your immediate conflict. If you sell windsocks in retail, for example, someone selling kites isn't directly competing with you, but they might still run across two or three encounters with the outside thing industry.

If you own a real store, you could even give a call to someone who works in a distant area and tell them you're in New York City and they're in Arizona. Either way, it makes sense that the internet is putting retailers on distant continents in jeopardy, so screw it. An alternative piece of advice would be to seek advice from someone at a larger company than yours who could be less likely to view you as a conflict.

Reach out to your industry. Prominent trade publications, your local business office, and your suppliers are excellent places to start for prospective trainers.

These are typically exceptional places for academics to visit, but how can you get someone who can facilitate with a style of their own? Seek a mentor in the same manner that people look for clinical experts or potential partners.

Reimburse mentors: But what if you had a brilliant idea that you wanted to implement right away and you needed a quick boost to your fitness level? Mind-blowingly comfortable mentorships develop gradually and can last for a very long period. If an accident programme is what you need, this might be the best opportunity to get qualified experts.

All stages of master advancement require the assistance of coaches. Firm visionaries use their tutor to help them think purposefully about the firm; presidents regularly use coaches to bounce ideas around; and coaches assist others in making difficult judgements. Think about the influence you can have if you volunteer to mentor your clients, agents, and accessories. You can instruct those around you and assist them in reaching their objectives more quickly. And easier. There are two main reasons why people look for coaches:

A few people in the group look for coaches to assist them in striking a balance between their personal and professional lives.

• Other people require tutors to aid them in growing their businesses or in sending their businesses.

People aren't searching for instant solutions anymore. They are looking for strategies to deal with pain and bring about change. The typically skilled expert does not actually accomplish the suffering transformation. A coach is a kind of master who helps clients consider long-lasting improvements of their own. The formative phase that goes along with guiding is called education. Teaching is a synthesis of business, finance, brain research, theory, power, and transformation. It assists people in gaining a clearer understanding of what they truly want out of life, be it career success, financial opportunity, educational relevance, individual achievement, genuine well-being, relationships, or calling arranging.

Chapter 3: Financial Planning

One crucial aspect of personal finance that might help you accumulate money over time is investing. Investing can help you attain long-term financial security, while saving can help you satisfy short-term financial goals.

Investment Types

Stocks, bonds, mutual funds, exchange-traded funds (ETFs), real estate, and other investment options are available. It's critical to conduct due diligence and select the appropriate investment kind for your needs, as each has pros and cons of its own.

Stocks represent ownership stakes in businesses. Purchasing stocks is akin to purchasing a tiny portion of that business. Although stocks can be a wise long-term investment, their value might change depending on the state of the market, making them somewhat hazardous.

Debt instruments issued by governments or businesses are called bonds. Purchasing a bond is equivalent to lending the issuer money. Although they usually give lesser returns than stocks, bonds are generally regarded as less hazardous.

For those who wish to invest in a range of securities but lack the time or experience to manage their portfolio, mutual funds can be a viable choice.

ETFs and mutual funds are comparable in that they are both collections of securities under the professional management of a fund manager. Nonetheless, they are more easily accessible and adaptable than mutual funds because they are exchanged on stock markets, much like individual equities.

Formulating a Plan for Investing

Making an investment plan is essential before you begin investing. This entails establishing a diversified portfolio, figuring out your investment objectives, and evaluating your risk tolerance.

Establishing your investment goals is the first stage in developing an investment plan. This could include accumulating long-term wealth, purchasing a home, or setting aside money for retirement. You may calculate how much money you need to invest and how long it will take to attain your goals once you've selected them.

When developing an investing plan, it's also critical to evaluate your level of risk tolerance. While some people choose to minimise risk and concentrate on more cautious investments, others are comfortable taking on more risk in exchange for the possibility of larger returns. Your unique financial condition and personal preferences will determine how much risk you can tolerate.

When investing, having a varied portfolio is also crucial. To lower risk, diversification entails distributing your investments among a variety of asset classes. This can offer a more consistent return over time and shield your portfolio from market fluctuations.

Investing Techniques

Among the several investment strategies available are value investing, aggressive investing, and passive investing.

like the S&P 500, is known as passive investing. This approach is frequently suggested for long-term investors who wish to reduce risk and concentrate on consistent, long-term gains.

Although this method can yield larger results, it can also be riskier and need more experience and knowledge.

Value investing is the process of identifying cheap stocks with long-term growth potential. Although this method necessitates extensive study and analysis, possibly larger returns may find it to be a viable option.

Whichever investing approach you decide on, it's critical to constantly assess and tweak your portfolio to make sure it matches your investment.

ADVICE FOR AN IDEAL FINANCIAL LIFE FREE FROM CRISIS

HABITATS Things to do

To prevent future financial difficulties, it is important to control spending and avoid impulsive purchases at the time of making purchases, among other fundamental aspects.

In addition to other advice, here are some money-saving strategies you can use if you'd like to have a savings reserve but haven't been able to:

1. Watch out where you save money— don't fall for a scam!

Some individuals may have been doing business with a specific bank for a long time and feel at ease doing so. which often makes them overpriced and detrimental to the customer's finances.

To find out if there are better possibilities for saving money in this situation, you will need to look up and review the policies of different banks.

2. It's okay to make conserving money one of your objectives!

Setting a goal and acknowledging the problem is the first step towards saving money. We must first make improvements to our goals because we frequently propose objectives that we are unable to accomplish in the future.

The primary strategy for saving money is to include it in your goals—perhaps with acquiring a wife or something else, if you get what I mean.

3. Establish a monthly savings goal.

You must go from the theoretical to the practical stage as soon as you decide to save money; that is, you must begin saving right away.

Even a tiny amount saved each month can help you save money, especially if your spending is planned out on a weekly basis.

4. Avoid using credit cards.

I would want to draw attention to the fact that while a credit card could be helpful for purchases, it can also lead to an inflated impression of the amount of money we actually spend. As a result, it is preferable to just leave the house with the cash you require as opposed to running up large credit card debt.

Compiling your monthly expenses and scheduling your monthly spending into a dedicated schedule is a smart step to take. Make it a challenge you face every day.

5. Evaluate your spending to see if it was financially worthwhile.

I may suggest that you should only purchase items that are necessary for you, like shoes, and not just because you find them appealing.

Waiting and considering your options carefully before making a purchase is a smart way to avoid buying needless things. You should weigh the benefits and drawbacks of any purchase and resist the temptation to buy something just because it looks nice. Be wise and resist the temptation to be drawn in by the discounts!

6. Keep the big picture in mind

If you only consider the short term, some people might not be willing to save money. However, if you consider the long term, it will be much easier, and you don't want to run into financial difficulties as you become older.

Along with many other crucial actions, saving money will be easier for you if you have a long-term perspective on life.

7. Use your customer card; don't be afraid to do so

It is usually a good idea to have one of these cards, especially if you go to the establishment frequently to purchase necessities. However, exercise caution, as this card may encourage you to make unnecessary purchases. Many establishments provide little discounts and presents to their patrons.

8. Have fun, and don't feel compelled to save

Though it's vital, saving money can occasionally feel like a chore. However, there are apps like "1Money" and "Spending Tracker" that make the process enjoyable and challenging.

9. Listening to music and chewing gum

You can reduce your impulsive consumption while you shop by chewing gum and wearing headphones, as many establishments employ scents or music to pique our interest. I know that sounds a little juvenile, but trust me—it works!

Managing Your Expenses

This book will teach you budgeting strategies and a variety of student loan repayment options that will make your student loan payments much more manageable. However, you must first determine whether you can now afford to make your student loan instalments. Why does this matter? Because I don't want you to fall behind on any of your student loans due to insufficient finances in the interim, even if it takes you a few weeks or longer to read this book.

And don't worry; the new SAVE repayment plan will be covered in the book very soon. Your payments can decrease by up to half next year.

But first, let's assess your performance on your student loan payments by having you complete this short quiz:

1. Are you able to pay back your student loans on schedule each month? __ yes __ no 2. Are you paying back all of your student loans? For guidance, return to the Personal Student Loan chart you made in Chapter 1. 3. Will paying your monthly student loan bills require you to take out a credit card debt or take money out of your savings account? __ yes __ no. __ yes __ no 4. Have you made any plans for how to prevent missing payments resulting from

inability to pay during the previous six months? __ in favour, __ against

If you said "yes" to questions 3 and 4 or "no" to questions 1 and 2, you need to take immediate action to improve your circumstances. Was the situation you're recovering from the brief? If so, you can explore your alternatives for repayment as you concentrate on making adjustments to your budget.

If things are still going on, you have two choices:

• You can take a week or two to examine your budget and consider choices like the SAVE Plan or an extended repayment plan if you can manage to make payments for a two- or three-month period. However, if you decide against an income-driven repayment plan at this point in your history, be sure you won't be eligible for any type of future forgiveness. Talk with your loan servicer about all of your alternatives.

If, even with the SAVE income-driven plan, you are unable to make your payments this year, you must contact your service provider right away to discuss income-based payment arrangements or temporary exemptions from payment obligations. You will have time to adjust your spending plan and consider all of your payment alternatives if you are granted a six-month temporary respite.

Whichever option you select, make sure all of the loans you still owe money on are included in the calculation by double-checking your Personal Student Loan chart. If you can afford all of your payments, you might assume you have plenty of time to consider your alternatives. However, you might find that you are only paying for four of the five loans.

AFFORDABILITY CHECKLIST FOR PAYMENTS

Assess if you are able to pay off your student loans in full each month without using up all of your money or using credit cards. If so, you will have more time to look over your budget and weigh your options for repayment. Act now to avoid a loan default if you are unable to make your instalments. Speak with your service provider about your alternatives right now.

Postponements and Patience

The most terrifying aspect of having any kind of recurrent debt is the possibility that you may one day lose your job or experience a wage cut to the point where you are unable to make the payments. In this particular area, student loans outperform credit card debt, auto loans, and mortgages because they come with an integrated forbearance and deferment programme that lets you skip payments in the event of a layoff or other financial emergency. You can use a deferment or forbearance to temporarily stop paying student loan payments, which will give you more time to sort things out.

Deferments are always preferable since they allow the government to cover the interest on your government-subsidized student loans. You will typically need to provide documentation to your lender proving your qualifying deferment circumstances, such as in the case of active duty military personnel, as the government must pay the interest.

While attending college, most of us did so part-time or with an unlimited deferment while in school. If we hadn't, and we hadn't paid, we most likely would have fallen behind before we could graduate.

To demonstrate that you meet the current requirements for this sort of postponement, you must provide proof of your income for economic deferments. Each loan programme has a maximum three-year economic deferment period. Visit http://studentaid.gov to get the most recent list of circumstances and requirements for deferment.

Additional frequent categories include unemployment, cancer treatment, Parent PLUS borrowers, military service, and post-active duty students.

Forbearances can be either mandatory or discretionary, and they are typically considerably easier to get than deferments.

A medical or dental internship, National Guard service, AmeriCorps service, involvement in the Department of Defence Student Debt Repayment Plan Programme, and teacher debt forgiveness are among the situations in which forbearances are required. If the amount you owe on your student loans exceeds twenty per cent of your gross monthly income, you might also be eligible.

Note: If you are considering forbearing, you should think about switching to an income-driven repayment schedule. You have the option of making payments of as little as $0, which will advance the maximum repayment period for your student loans.

The servicer has the final say over general forbearance decisions. If you are unable to qualify for economic deferment due to a temporary financial hardship, you may be eligible for general forbearance.

There are two sides to the general forbearance story. Forbearance periods were previously limited to three years, but now the servicer can provide approval for as long as necessary.

Explaining your financial circumstances and inquiring about other possibilities, such as income-based repayment or perhaps enrolling in an extended repayment plan, is the best course of action.

For instance, suppose you're barely making ends meet paycheck to paycheck. Right now, taking a break from your student loan payments would be quite beneficial. Thus, you agree to forbearance throughout the entire three-year period. Your income increases, and your knowledge of budgeting improves. You can use the extra cash you're receiving to upgrade your flat, go out with friends, and buy a new automobile. However, the initial $40,000 in student loans at a 6% interest rate has increased to $47,640 by the conclusion of the three years.

Would you have been better off making your student loan payments while just scraping by for a few months or a year?

CHAPTER 10: SUCCESS METHODS: ADHERING TO YOUR

Maintaining discipline, motivation, and consistency in your spending patterns is necessary. We'll go over some practical methods in this chapter to support you in sticking to your budget and reaching your financial objectives.

Establish sensible objectives

Establishing attainable financial objectives helps support your budgeting approach and keep you motivated. It is crucial to divide your financial objectives into more manageable, smaller benchmarks.

Monitor Your Expenses

Maintaining a budget requires careful monitoring of your spending. It will assist you in locating areas where you are overspending and reducing wasteful spending. There are other approaches to keeping tabs on your expenses, such as making a spreadsheet or using apps for budgeting. You can make changes to your budget to make sure you stay on track after you understand where your money is going.

Cash Is Better Than Credit Cards

Sticking to your spending plan is made easier when you use cash rather than credit cards. However, using credit cards can result in impulsive purchases and debt accumulation, which makes it challenging to follow a budget.

Automate Your Saves Keeping up with your budgeting plan can be achieved in part by automating your savings. You may guarantee that you save a certain amount every month by setting up automatic transfers. Additionally, it will assist you in resisting the need to spend the money you had planned to preserve.

Steer clear of temptations.

Adhering to your budget requires avoiding temptations. It can entail steering clear of internet retailers or the mall. Finding strategies to prevent the triggers that lead to overspending is also crucial. For instance, if you tend to overspend when you're under stress, look for other non-financial coping mechanisms.

Examine and Modify Your Budget

Staying on track requires routinely reviewing and revising your budget. It's critical to frequently evaluate your spending patterns and, if needed, change your budget. Life events like job loss, medical difficulties, or unforeseen costs may impact your budget. You can make sure that you keep on track in spite of these occurrences by routinely evaluating and modifying your budget.

It takes ambition and discipline to follow a budget. Setting realistic goals, keeping an eye on your spending, avoiding temptations, automating saves, using cash instead of credit cards, and routinely reviewing and adjusting your budget are all crucial. You can stick to your budget and meet your financial objectives by using these techniques.

Establishing A Strong Bankround

Completing your long-term financial goals and safeguarding your financial future requires building a solid financial foundation. Here's what you should know whether you're just embarking on your financial journey or hoping to improve your current financial situation: 1. Make a financial plan by tracking your expenses and income first. A simple tool that might help you make wise financial decisions is a spending plan, which shows you where your money is going.

Enumerate all of your sources of income and arrange your expenses, encompassing housing, travel, groceries, utilities, and entertainment. Make sure your expenses don't exceed your income.

2. Regular Savings: One of the most important steps in achieving financial security is saving money. Set aside a portion of your money on a regular basis, even if it's only a small amount.Once that's in place, focus on saving for both your immediate and long-term goals.

3. Pay-Off Obligation: One of the biggest obstacles to financial soundness might be hefty interest commitments. You'll have more money available for savings

and investments as you settle your debts.

4. Create a Just-in-case account: Having a hidden fund is essential because life is full of unexpected events. This means to save, on an open record, approximately three to five years' worth of daily expenses. This will provide you with a safety net in the event that there are job layoffs or unexpected expenses.

5. Invest Wisely: After paying off high-interest debt, consider investing your money to increase your wealth over time. To reduce risk, spread your investments throughout. Seek guidance from a financial consultant for tailored advice.

6. Make a Retirement Plan: Retirement savings should be a top priority.establish individual retirement accounts (IRAs). The longer your investments take to grow, the sooner you should start saving for retirement.

7. Safeguard Your Resources: Always keep safety in mind. Make sure you have enough health, vehicle, and house insurance to secure your assets and offer financial stability in the event of unanticipated events.

8. Always Be Learning: Developing financial literacy requires constant contact. Keep up with topics related to personal finance, investing, and tax preparation. The greater your

knowledge, the more equipped you will be to make wise financial decisions.

9. Establish Explicit Financial Goals: Having definite financial goals can help you stay focused and convinced about your financial journey. whether you're buying a house, starting a family, or travelling to far-off places.

10. Evaluate and Adjust: Regularly assess your financial plan and adjust as necessary. Your financial plan should adapt to the changes in your life.

Generating Practical Money Concepts,

Once limiting beliefs have been identified, swap them out for positive ones that support long-term objectives. Limiting beliefs are easily changed by questioning their integrity, analysing how they shape your present identity, and addressing your apprehensions about how new concepts can impact your life.

Prepare yourself to simultaneously let go of beliefs that hold you back from reaching your objectives.

If you discover, for example, that you think, "People like me never get rich," you may define "people like me" and then read about the lives of people who have achieved financially by exhibiting similar characteristics, which would challenge your underlying view. You might also consider how clinging to the restrictive notion shields your identity, provides a justification for maintaining your current financial situation, and keeps you from having to cope with the effects of change.

Novel perspectives and the identity component. Identity always emerges because of the exterior modifications that beliefs create, especially with regard to conduct. Determination, confusion, and a lack of confidence might arise from not knowing what to expect or how to respond. You can build the resilience you need to forge a new financial identity by foreseeing these disruptions and contacting like-minded individuals or prosperity buddies.

..Rather than be bewildered by an uncontrollably large credit card statement, I would much rather realise that I've exceeded my vacation budget and make necessary adjustments elsewhere.

Conserving

We can create virtuous habits! Embrace saving as a way of life. As they say in the traditional classic, pay yourself first. Every time, before you do anything else, set aside some money from your salary for yourself.

Treat yourself first and tell yourself you deserve the money before you pay the other bills.

Analyse your expenditures carefully as well. Cut off any product or item that turns out to be unnecessary, and live your life the way someone else would run their business.

The money you would have saved by giving up your $4 cup of coffee a day would add up over time.

Some people are very careful with their money. Individuals are more prone to be self-centred and unmotivated to assist others.

Do we have to spend money? Of course, to maintain the currency's circulation. In addition, we want to be able to enjoy life if we don't completely appreciate it and debt collectors keep contacting.

They can be very annoying, as I can confirm. A large percentage of the stuff we purchase with our goods is redundant or offers very little value to our lives.

Managing Debt: Definition and Handling

If you take out a loan from someone or a business, you have debt. You have to pay back the money you owe, sometimes in instalments that are set.

You usually use the money from your next salary to make those payments.

Even though you could be able to get anything right away with a loan, you can be stuck with monthly payments for a few months or even a few years.

Debt is not the same as credit. Credit can be obtained even if you have no debt. For example, you may have a credit card that is completely paid off.

• Determine what is and is not necessary.

Another thing that most students struggle with is telling the difference between their needs and wants. Some students waste their money on items that are just a waste since they don't know the difference between essential and non-essential.

For daily living, necessities, including food, clothing, and hygiene products, are required. Conversely, if you already have numerous teams, non-essential items can be things like electrical devices, a movie outing, or a pair of shoes. Restricting your spending is essential because it will help you cut out goods that you don't need for your budget, even though it may be difficult at first.

• Cutting the price of specific supplies.

It could be easy to save money on supplies, particularly if you live on campus. You could look around the nearby bookshops to see if they are much less expensive before walking straight to the campus bookstore. You might be able to save money on the textbooks you need for the upcoming semester by doing this. Furthermore, if you choose to download your book to an e-reader or tablet, you could be able to save even more money. If you are attempting to hold onto specific items, such as loose-leaf paper and 3-ring binders, think about purchasing in bulk from a company that offers

office equipment. Shops give you a discount if you purchase a large amount of merchandise. Try websites in case all else fails. This could help you find bargains and save money.

Finally.

Having wise spending habits can be difficult to achieve. On the other hand, you might benefit from this in the long run. If you're new to handling your finances, the methods mentioned above could save you a tonne of time. Avoid places that encourage you to buy items that are not necessary for your daily life if you are unable to manage your expenses effectively. Be aware that knowing what you need and what you want is not the same thing. Therefore, manage your finances wisely while you're in school so that you can accumulate a large sum of money that you can utilise for other important goals or future expenses.

Understand How to Set and Reach Goals

Discover the appropriate way to communicate while setting financial goals. As stated by the acronym SMART, objectives should be clear, measurable, attainable, realistic, and time-sensitive. Record your goals as well as the steps you need to take to reach them.

That you plan for in your calendar.

Find Out Whether You Should Buy or Rent

You might be shocked to learn that not everyone is financially suited to purchase a home. For some people, renting is a far better option. This is especially clear in the unlikely event that you are unsure of where you will need to live over the next five to ten years. Leasing can also make your life better because you won't be responsible for unplanned repairs.

Increase Your Passive Income Streams

Studies reveal that the majority of wealthy people experience frequent wage spikes. Whether or not you worry about being "rich," the fact remains that having a second source of income can really help you out financially. These days, there are several ways to generate automated income, ranging from online sales of premium and member goods to rental speculations.

Put Learning on Hold and Get Into Action

If you've read a lot about money but are now struggling to implement what you've learned, heed this advice and go for it. Execute an action. Select a specific item and only share it completely. Once you've achieved that, you'll feel as though you should take the next action. Taking control of your finances is more about making the most of what you already have than it is about learning to live without. In actuality, financial problems are frequently just the result of not giving the matter enough thought.

It will be much more difficult to improve your life if you frequently buy espresso at the shop every day, go out to eat without making any plans, and are clueless about how much you owe or acquire. Either way, it will be much easier to make ends meet if you know what you have, what's coming in, what's going out, and why and how.

Techniques for Saying No

People's inability to say no is one reason they often feel dominated at work and home. A significant amount of this is planned socialisation meant to create amazing working drones in the public sphere. Still, in reality, all it does is cause people to overcommit to life and do more than is necessary. You really can say what you say and probably should. This is the path.

First, ask yourself these three questions:

1. Does it align with my strengths?

2. Do I really have this chance?

3. Do I really think that should be the case?

If the answer to any of these questions is no, you should just say so. It's not necessary to answer negatively on each of the three counts. You can just say no if you would prefer not to say yes. Either way, there are often a variety of causes.

Not Clearly Needed for an Explanation

By all means, there's no need for an explanation. Saying no is an easy option. Without additional context, "no" is a complete and whole statement. You are free to explain, but going overboard is not necessary. Some "no sentences" that you can use in the case that necessary are listed below.

> "Goodness, thank you for asking. However, it is basically impossible that I can make it work at present."

> "Please accept my apologies, yet I can't do that since it conflicts with my strict perspective; however, gratitude for inquiring."

> "Much thanks to you for asking, yet I am not the perfect individual for this work. Have you considered asking Amy if this is truly right up her alley?"

> "Not at the present time. I as of now have needs booked for that day and time. Much thanks to you."

> "I can't do that, yet in the event that you can do this, then I can do it this way as of now."

Practice pronouncing these sentences and add a sentence of your own that you may use.

You are likely now being asked to complete tasks. It's possible that you should have said no when you said OK. For the next time, practise saying no.

Give Up Your Blame

Remember how saying no used to make you feel awful in your early years? It's only that since you were two years old, your mother has always said "NO!" whenever you tried to reach that lovely jar, and you may associate NO with something terrible. Everybody experiences it. However, you can say no to anyone about anything, just as your mother had to understandably say no to you.

Things without feeling guilty. If you say no in a deliberate way, you'll never have an excuse to feel bad about it. Time is something you should protect because it's so precious. Take on tasks that you genuinely need to undertake, that you have the energy to complete, and that you genuinely trust in.

Detailed steps on letting go of negative people

Similar to how saying no makes things better, as you look back on your life, you may discover that you also need to let go of detrimental people from your daily routine. Those who are poisonous will usually put on quite a show for those in their relationships. There's always something to be grateful for when your life shows less.

Day Eleven

D

Debt can take many different forms, including credit card balances, medical expenses, student loans, mortgages, auto loans, and personal loans from friends or family.

I'm assuming you have one or more debts (or maybe three or four) that occasionally give you the willies at night or during the day since you're not sure how you're going to pay them off.

Yes, that is precisely what we will examine over the following four days. You cannot truly eliminate debt from your life by continuing to ignore it or take a passive approach to it. It won't go away or stop you from thinking about it if you run away from it, don't make any statements, or sweep everything under the rug. This behaviour only serves to make you suppress your thoughts and feelings about your debt rather than using them to help you plan how to pay it off. This causes the debt to linger beneath the surface, which in turn causes stress and anxiety because you are unsure of how to deal with it or how to take proactive steps to find a solution.

If you've ever believed that living debt-free is unachievable, you'd better get used to the fact that this is your goal going forward. The days of burying your head in the sand and refusing to face your debt or without a strategy to pay it off are long gone. Let's start with your existing circumstances and determine how much debt you have in order to get there.

As you compile a complete picture of your debts, make sure to include everything. Add all of the money you owe other people, including modest loans from family or personal debts.

Action Plan for Day 11

Recognise your debts.

Gather statement information from all outstanding debts. To find out the current amounts, locate the most recent paper statement, sign into your account, or get in touch with the organisation you owe money to. Some of this information may have been acquired in order to determine your net worth on day ten.

Make a list of all of your debts and include information about their minimum monthly payments, interest rates, remaining terms, and outstanding balances.

Examine the items on your list. Let all of your emotions and ideas run through you for a minute. They could be worries related to your spending patterns, concerns about how you will pay these off, alarm at the amount you owe, relief about how small it is, enthusiasm about deciding to finally get rid of them from your life, or anything else.

All of that for now. We'll discuss what to do next on day 12, but for now, enjoy a small treat and know that you've made a significant first step towards being debt-free.

ACT HONOURABLE

The greatest salespeople throughout history, in my opinion, have always spoken the truth. But there's nothing at all wrong with a little spin; you have to emphasize the advantages of a product in order to sell it. Honesty and morality are the cornerstones of selling. Online evaluations on third-party websites are replacing the traditional practice of customers taking whatever they get from the company. Here, customers hold businesses accountable and are eager to point out flaws and weaknesses in products.

You don't want to receive negative feedback from such assessments.

Being honest about your intentions is essential if you want customers to compliment your items.

Consumers anticipate receiving sales from you.

They don't mind entering into the transaction with the knowledge that your business exists to sell things since they expect to pay a fair price for a fair product. Some sales techniques adhere to the context of ethical selling. Customers anticipate seeing them, and trying to sell as much as possible is not a betrayal of integrity.

An excellent illustration is what's known as upselling. A straightforward instance of upselling would be if a fast-food restaurant asked you if you would want fries with that. There is no moral problem with reminding a customer of another product you have that might be a better fit for his needs, even if it is more expensive; if you have already sold him a product and at some point throughout the sales process, you offer another one that is somewhat more expensive but has more benefits. Offering a different product from your line in addition to the one the customer just purchased is not morally wrong if you genuinely think your product solves their difficulties.

Similarly, it's always OK to down-sell or present a customer with a fantastic offer in the event that they turn down your initial offer. Let's say the customer shows interest in your offerings but isn't willing to part with the cash. Is there a different product you could provide that would satisfy their requirements at a lower cost? Offering a product at a lower cost is perfectly acceptable if that is the true problem. All you're doing is presenting an alternative that they might choose to embrace or reject.

When making an online purchase, consider your reaction and yourself at all times.

To what extent are you willing to click on an offer even after receiving pop-up boxes before getting annoyed? Although there is a wide range of opinions among internet marketers, the majority of ethical marketers concur that one or two pop-up boxes are acceptable. However, after that, there is a greater chance of frustration as the visitor to your website tries to leave but is consistently prevented from doing so. Say you are in a store, and you have made the decision not to purchase anything today. What would happen if the salesperson prevented you from opening the door? What would your thoughts be on the store's owner? That's precisely the thought you want to avoid giving your prospective client.

You must permit someone to click away from your offer if they so want. You might permanently lose a consumer if you block the door.

Being truthful goes a long way in the modern world when individuals make all kinds of claims about their goods and services.

Section 3. Could I Get a Score of "800+"?

Maintain Savings

It's time for the challenging phase now. Perhaps you have been following along with some of the tasks in this guidebook, and your FICO score has increased noticeably.

Although this is always wonderful news, let's see if we can raise our score to 800 or above. This type of score is exclusive to the top. It is challenging to obtain since it necessitates, among other things, a high credit limit, an ideal mix of credit types, and no late payments. However, it is conceivable.

It is much simpler for you to apply for credit and loans whenever you want when your credit score is this good. This credit score can assist you in handling several medical expenditures in the event of an emergency. It can also be utilized for non-emergency situations, such as when you want to buy a new home, launch a business, or take on another similar project.

How can you ensure that your credit score reaches 800 or above? Understanding the facts is the first step. After you are able to respond to the primary query, "What is a perfect credit score? You'll discover that it is simpler to take the appropriate actions to determine exactly what you need to accomplish in order to receive the highest possible score. To begin with, though, you must confirm your position on the FICO scale.

You can obtain a free yearly credit report from each of the three major credit bureaus in the nation once a year. This is the moment to address any problems you uncover if you go through this and discover any of them (sometimes, a mistake will appear on one and not on the others). If your report contains a lot of faults, you will never be able to achieve an 800+ score.

Creating a lengthy credit history is the next area of concentration.

Lenders generally often consider borrowers with short credit histories to be riskier to work with. However, there may be some exceptions. You must first build and then continue to maintain a lengthy credit history in order to obtain a credit score of 800 or higher. Keeping some of the accounts open will help you improve your score even if you are not using them.

You have to make sure that all of your payments are paid on time, as we have touched on a few times. Nobody with a credit score of 800 or more has ever had a missed payment—or several missed payments—on their record. If you find it difficult to remember when things are due, you might want to set up automated payments to take care of that for you.

It's also important that you take the time to reconsider how you use credit cards. Although we often want to stay around 30 per cent, it's ideal to stay under 10 per cent if you're aiming for a higher score.

Although it hasn't been covered much in this article, learning how to diversify the accounts you are holding onto will help you achieve the better score you desire. While it may take some time to complete, this is one of the best methods to build your credit, and it's a wonderful way for us to ensure that your credit score can rise.

Diversifying your accounts can help you raise your credit score. This does not give you permission to go out and get ten credit card accounts at once. It implies that you ought to have a variety of credit, including credit cards, mortgages, school loans, and auto loans.

Ten credit cards won't demonstrate responsibility with your score or be a varied mix of debt. However, it will be far more convenient to deal with numerous accounts, even if some of them have been paid off.

Make sure you reduce your expenses and establish a budget you can keep to while you concentrate on improving your credit score. This lessens the likelihood that your spending will get out of control and helps you stay within your means. Living within your means is a wonderful method to improve your credit score, even though your income will not be taken into account by your credit score.

Finding strategies to reduce the liability you are facing is the next item on the list. It may sound pleasant to cosign a loan but keep in mind that you are taking on another person's risk when you do so. You will be held accountable for that debt as well, so doing this for someone who struggles to manage their debt will hurt your credit score. Avoid cosigning anything at all if you want to ensure that you can obtain and keep a credit score of at least 800.

Furthermore, you want to confirm that your responsibility is restricted in other ways as well. Cards that have been lost or stolen should always be reported as soon as possible. In the event that you fail to take this action, you may find yourself accountable for any purchases that were not approved at the time. Your score will be negatively impacted in this situation if you are unable to make those transactions.

Lastly, you must ensure that the harsh questions that are made about your report are limited. You are handling a query, whether it comes from you or another organization or agency requesting a copy of the credit report. Occasionally, a soft inquiry may occur, but it usually won't be sufficient to modify your credit. One of the following events will trigger this gentle inquiry:

You review and investigate your credit report.

You grant authorization to a prospective employer to review and verify your credit.

The financial institutions you deal with are required to run credit checks on you.

Once you receive a preapproved credit card offer, the particular business investigates your credit.

You should exercise caution when it comes to the hard inquiry, even though the soft inquiry won't have a significant impact on your credit ratings. This is the one that has the potential to impact your credit score. This is the process by which a business obtains your credit report subsequent to your application for a loan or credit card. To achieve the best outcomes with this, you want to make sure that you can minimize the number of harsh queries.

Get Rid of Procrastination

Releasing yourself from the constraints of indecision and delay by quitting procrastination is akin to freeing your productivity. It entails admitting that the task at hand demands your attention, regardless of how difficult or distasteful it may be. Dividing the work into more manageable, smaller subtasks is a useful tactic. By taking on these little tasks one at a time, you may reduce the task's seemingly intimidating size and experience a sense of accomplishment as you finish each one. Discovering the causes of your procrastination can also be illuminating. It could be a lack of drive, a fear of failing, or simply an unclear course of action. Overcoming procrastination requires addressing these underlying problems, establishing specific goals, and encouraging self-discipline. The satisfaction of finishing chores is the reward for beating procrastination.

Moreover, overcoming procrastination can be greatly aided by an organized strategy. A sense of urgency and accountability can be instilled by using time management strategies like the Pomodoro Technique or Time Blocking, as well as by using to-do lists and deadlines. Good habits can also be reinforced by creating a routine that incorporates these techniques and reflecting on your development on a regular basis. We can all struggle with procrastination, but with deliberate effort, awareness, and a systematic approach, we can overcome it and reach our greatest potential for achieving our objectives.

Using the Two-Minute Rule to Overcome

Using the Two-Minute Rule to combat overwhelm is a game-changing tactic that clears your head and your to-do list. This rule is based on the idea that it is more productive to accomplish a task right away rather than putting it off if it takes less than two minutes to finish. You keep these short and frequently insignificant jobs from building up and creating mental strain by taking care of them quickly. Whether it's answering an email, arranging your workspace, or having a quick phone conversation, jumping on things that take two minutes or less can free up time on your schedule and give you a sense of success. This proactive strategy provides a clear way to remain on top of your commitments and retain a feeling of order in the chaos of a busy day by ensuring that tiny activities don't compound into greater stressors.

Section Four

ETHICAL WORK-LIFE BALANCE

The Value of Personal Care

It is impossible to overstate the importance of self-care; it is the cornerstone of a prosperous, healthy, and fulfilling life. The term "self-care" describes a wide range of intentional actions and routines meant to enhance your mental, emotional, physical, and spiritual health. It's a need, much like filling up your car with petrol before a long drive, not a luxury. Making self-care a priority is essentially an investment in yourself because it will recharge your resilience, energy, and overall vitality.

Self-care is, first and foremost, essential to preserving excellent physical health. It entails healthy eating, consistent exercise, enough sleep, and hygiene. chance of developing chronic illnesses, and live longer when you take good care of your body. Physical self-care also includes preventive actions like routine screenings and check-ups, which guarantee that any possible health problems are identified and treated as soon as possible.

It is impossible to exaggerate the significance of emotional self-care. Getting support when needed, processing your emotions, and partaking in enjoyable and relaxing activities are all steps towards achieving a healthy emotional state. Self-reflection, therapy, pastimes, quality time with loved ones, and engaging in activities that evoke strong feelings are all examples of emotional self-care.

Taking part in mentally stimulating and enlightening activities is a form of mental self-care. Mental self-care includes reading, writing, thinking critically, solving problems, and practising mindfulness. This also includes creating realistic goals, arranging your thoughts, and taking breaks to clear your head. Maintaining cognitive health, improving focus, and encouraging an optimistic outlook are all aspects of mental self-care.

It's about taking care of your soul, developing inner peace, and trying to live in harmony with your environment.

To be more precise, balance is what self-care is all about. It involves being aware of, listening to, and attending to the needs of your body, mind, and spirit. Self-care on a regular basis helps you restock your resources and improve your ability to serve others, both personally and professionally. Recall that taking care of yourself is an essential investment in your general well-being that will enable you to manifest your best self in all spheres of your life. It is not selfishness.

Advice Nos. 21–25

21. The objective is to make as much money as you can.

Your earning ability is the key to achieving any financial goal, even financial freedom. In your profession or career, you have to aim for maximum profit and make as much money as you can. If you follow through, this money will help you realize your goal of becoming financially independent.

22. Recognize When to Collect Debts

Taking charge of your finances is the first step in the process of becoming financially free. Having an emergency fund, even if it's only $1,000 or three months' worth of living expenses, is essential once you've created a budget. You then have to pay off any small bills, with the exception of your mortgage. Having no debt is beneficial for money.

23. Remain Debt-Free After You're There.

Declare that you will never take on debt again after you have paid off all of your small obligations. Set aside money in your budget for exclusively cash purchases. Cut up every credit card you own. Use a debit card or buy a credit card and load it with the necessary money before using it if you must use a credit card when travelling.

24- Define Long-Term Financial Objectives

an emergency fund are the two main goals on the road to financial independence. After achieving those objectives, you should decide on your long-term financial objectives. These are your desired outcomes for the next 10, twenty, and more years.

25. Use Your Time and Talent Creatively

You may have a skill that could earn you additional money. Evaluate the services you can provide. There are many good materials available on the internet. To meet your financial objectives more quickly, look for other sources of income. Allocate a few hours every week to this task and begin achieving financial independence.

Advice Nos. 26–30

26. Keep in Mind That You Must Allow for Taxes

Even if you become financially and debt-free, taxes will still need to be paid. Never forget to account for the tax bill— it will arrive. You will discover that you will have to pay more taxes as you become more financially independent. Rather than being shocked by it, prepare for it in advance. Consult a tax professional beforehand.

27. Compile detailed daily schedules.

You should plan for each day as well as the upcoming month, as you have various recommendations for doing so. You'll be able to avoid financial surprises and maintain your budget with this. Simply review each day the day before to ensure that everything you require fits inside your spending limit. It's worth it and should just take five or ten minutes.

28. Assemble Supplies Based on the Seasons

Even though it could be tempting to hoard items when they're out of season, you should concentrate on the current season. This is particularly valid if you are cramped. Make good use of your space. If you are going to experience a period of lower income, prepare for it in advance to lessen the impact on you. Follow along with what's coming up next season.

29. Make Your Bank Accounts More Efficient

You should take this action as soon as possible on your path to financial independence. Examine each of your accounts, and when requesting a discount, try to maximize them as well. Switching to an interest-bearing account is advised if your checking account balance is $1,000 or higher. Seek out incentives and work to get your interest rates lowered.

30-Financial Merger

Wherever it is feasible, you should think about consolidating your debt as you strive to become debt-free. To pay off the higher-interest debt, you can try applying for a loan with a reduced interest rate. You might apply for a credit card with a reduced interest rate and transfer your existing credit card debt onto it. You can use the extra money to pay off the debt in full thanks to the interest rate savings.

MANAGE YOUR MONEY AND ENSURE IT PRODUCES MORE EARNINGS FOR YOU.

Developing a few wise habits could be the key to financial mastery. Indeed, "Habits are the source of riches, poverty,happiness,despair,stress, good relationships, poor relationships, good health, or ill health."

These simple personal finance techniques will help you make your accounts overflow; you can start implementing them right now.

Set up financial automation.

One self-made billionaire, David Bach, advises you to make urgent changes to your financial strategy if it isn't already automated. Putting money into savings, investments, and other accounts automatically is known as financial automation.

Creditors—makes it easy for you to accumulate riches.

According to Bach, it's "the one step that nearly assures that you won't fail financially."

"The Automatic Millionaire." "You'll never miss a payment again—and you'll never be tempted to scrimp on savings since you won't even see the money travelling straight from your paycheck to your savings accounts."

Just link your accounts, designate the exact day you wish to start transfers, and watch as money from your paycheck appears directly in your savings account.

Automation "frees up important time and enables you to concentrate on the good things of life, rather than wasting time worrying about whether you paid that bill or whether you're going to overspend," in addition to ensuring that you never make a late payment again.

Put money into your "spare income."

Extra money shouldn't be left unused. in contrast to popular belief, you don't need a large initial investment to get started.

Initiate investments as soon as possible to fully capitalise on compound interest. A small investment can provide a large lifetime return if you make wise investments.

Establish definite financial goals.

Clearly state the responsibilities and goals for every dollar you spend. Set goals for your annual income and net worth in writing. As with creating any kind of goal, keep things reasonable, but don't be scared to push yourself.

In addition, having big dreams is one way to become affluent.

Save unexpected money; don't waste it.

Act as though there is no more money—a bonus, a cheque for your birthday or any other windfall. Make it a habit to deposit any unforeseen funds, regardless of the amount—even a $20 bill you discover in your coat pocket—at the bank. Use it for debt, investments, emergency savings, or student loans. Everything will come together.

Moreover, if you start this habit early on, it will assist you in avoiding lifestyle inflation in the event of an unexpected rise or additional money.

Remind yourself that you are deserving of success.

In his book "How Rich People Think," self-made billionaire Steve Siebold states that "success, contentment, and pleasure are the natural ordering of life" for the wealthiest people.

The outstanding ones are driven by a single conviction to take actions that almost guarantee victory."

However, the average salary continues to be ordinary since that is what people anticipate. "The majority believe they aren't deserving of big fortune," the self-made billionaire claims. "They question themselves, asking who am I to become a millionaire?" You could try asking yourself, "Why not me? That's what millionaires and billionaires do, after all.

Read for at least thirty minutes each day. Even after your official education ends, you should keep investing in and training yourself. This will provide you with the knowledge and skills necessary to become more successful and make wise investments. Researching a company in-depth before making a financial commitment protects you from losing money.

Be in the company of prosperous people. Your financial worth tends to resemble that of your closest friends, so who you hang out with matters more than you might think.

Rich people usually believe that awareness spreads like wildfire and that meeting other successful people can broaden your perspective and increase your income.

Keep tabs on your bills and expenses.

You can't create wealth if you're spending more money than you're making. To ensure that you're making more than you're spending, keep track of your daily expenses. You can use a spreadsheet on your computer or simply jot down your daily purchases in a notepad or on your phone.

It's also critical to understand that not all debt is created equal. One great strategy is to list all of your debts in order of interest rate. making minimum payments on all of your other obligations to reduce your total loan lifetime interest costs.

The most important thing is to get out of the red as quickly as possible because it's difficult to start saving money when you're in debt.

Credit-Based Cards

I was convinced that I would never take advantage of my life or own a Visa because of the terrifying stories I had heard since I was a teenager. I saw credit as Satan and obligation as the enemy. I had witnessed people and abundance being destroyed to pay off debtors and

Mastercards. One day, while I was talking with a friend at my B-school, he showed me the other side of advances and charge cards. I can honestly say that this experience completely upended my beliefs, ideas, and judgements.

He said that Mastercards are free money! Free means that you can use all of the Visa's limit at the beginning and then pay the bill on the 48th day or on the due date specified on your card, which is usually around 1.5 months. This means that you can spend the money you don't have at 0% premium expense and increase this cycle by 10 to multiple times on a regular basis. You have free money all year long while your own money, whether it be business or compensation pay, is kept safe in the bank or possibly a flexible asset that receives 4 to 7% of the premium on the base. The possible outcome here is that should you fail to pay the money within the allotted time; you should pay 4 to multiple times the amount that you have earned.

One easy way to get 2% more is to keep all of your cash in an obligation store or fluid asset, which pays 2–4% more than your bank financing costs. You can then opt for an auto-charge into your investment account, from which you can choose to opt for an auto-charge into your Visa bill payment. Another simple way to do this is to keep cash in your ledger equal to your charge card limit and to pick in for an auto-charge office only two or three days before your charging cycle.

Even though the second option is a little more involved, it's merely a one-time practice that you really want to carry out. After all the frameworks are in place, you won't ever default (as long as your bank balance remains stable), and the average 4 to 7% return would truly become risk-free.

Additional Advantages:

1. restrictions: One further excellent argument for obtaining a Mastercard is the availability of restrictions on a variety of items, such as groceries.

Fuel, and various other daily necessities. Websites such as Amazon and

Flipkartprovide a clear 1-2% discount on specific Mastercard. Additionally, there are certain Mastercards that are restricted by Indian Oil and BPCL to provide 70-100 litres of free fuel or diesel.

2. Cashbacks: Banks and credit card companies give level cashback on a certain amount of spending. The idea is to gradually make people dependent on spending to the point where people are unable to pay their bills and are caught in an endless cycle of interest. This is the general reason that credit card companies start making real profits. However, if we can manage our spending, stay well within our means, and take advantage of all the cashback,

we will be better off than if we didn't have a credit card. As a result, this is also free money that we can extract by just altering the way we make payments.

3. Reward points: Another important argument in favour of choosing a Mastercard is that credit cards provide points that can be redeemed at various locations. Occasionally, these points combine with cashback and available limits, but occasionally they stand alone. For example, if you receive some Sodexo points and you can use them to buy food, that would be a great way to save money.

4. The airport advantage: When combined with your regular flight expenses, charge cards provide a

reasonable benefit. For example, my Kotak Debit card offered free accommodations for ticket appointments on almost all carriers. Last year, I must have booked about 15 tickets; even if we deduct an average convenience fee of ₹ 250, that still means I saved ₹ 3750. Most charge cards come with free parlour access, free food at the parlours, and preferred customer credits that accumulate and can be converted into tickets whenever needed. The financial benefits of charge cards can total up to ₹ 10,000 annually, assuming they are used wisely. Additionally, Visas provide flight protection and credit.

5. Safety: Unlike a cheque card, which allows you to withdraw all of your

available funds with a single click, credit cards have a cutoff to the harm they can do you. This protects your ledger from extortion and allows you to use them openly in questionable locations.

6. Credit score: Lastly, Mastercards help you create a FICO score, which

can be used at a later time when you need to take advantage of a large advance for housing or that expensive car. On-time Mastercard instalments show your creditworthiness to the lender and establish you as a reliable borrower. This can help you advance and arrange the loan costs when you apply for a larger loan.

A Guide to Personal Finances: Budgeting and Management

Section Two

2.1.2 How Can You Manage Your Money Efficiently? Keep tabs on your income and outgoing expenses. There are plenty of online cost trackers available.

If you don't want to utilise them, you can use a basic Google Spreadsheet or Excel Sheet. When you can see your expenses, you can examine how you spend your money and learn what is and isn't necessary.

Use credit cards wisely; avoid going overboard. We will cover how to manage your money well in a later part. Personal or business loans will certainly cover some gaps, but if they are not repaid responsibly, they become a never-ending cycle of debt.

The best course of action is to put your income into an action plan and try to allocate it according to demands, wants, necessities, personal activities, etc.

Make the most of your leisure time. Educate yourself on personal finance. The world of finance may seem overwhelming at first, but once you dive in, you'll start to develop your abilities and gain greater financial security. So, let's dive in and learn how to eliminate debt.

Another factor that could affect your monthly budget is student loans. Some income-based repayment plans cap your payments at 10% to 15% of your income, which is a safe amount but often results in payments stretching over several years and costing you a small fortune in rent adjustments. Try allocating 20% of your budget, especially if you don't have a car payment or are sharing rent with roommates.

Additional recommended percentages for continuous costs consist of utilities (10%), food (10–15%), and savings (10–15%).

Taking Your Budget

The best way to achieve this is to make an annual plan that accounts for your fixed costs, such as rent and car payments; your annual costs, such as holiday rentals and vacations; and your discretionary costs, such as dining out and clothing purchases. Combine all of these into a 12-month plan and stick to it.

You can adjust the plan if you find holes in it or your cash flow changes, but if you decide to stick with it, consider using budgeting software or apps to assist you. If you do it on your own, you'll be surprised when your debts are paid off, your savings increase and your requirements are met.

12 Habits to Help You Achieve Financial Freedom: Step-by-Step Guide

With these 12 tendencies, you'll lay the path to freedom from the rat race before you know it.

Independence from the rat race means having enough savings, investments, and cash on hand to cover the costs of the lifestyle you require for yourself and your family. It also means building up a savings account large enough to allow you to leave your job or pursue any career you desire without feeling pressured to accumulate a certain amount of money each year.

Sadly, too many people fall short of their goal of being free of the rat race. In fact, even in the absence of occasional financial crises. When a major emergency completely upends plans, such as a tropical storm, earthquake, or pandemic, more gaps in safety nets are revealed.

Almost everyone experiences inconvenience, yet these 12 tendencies might help you go in the right direction.

ESSENTIAL NOTES

Describe your life goals, including financial and lifestyle goals of all kinds, and create a plan for achieving them.

Handle Mastercards completely, assign as little responsibility as possible, and keep an eye on your FICO score.

Create scheduled investing funds by contributing to your manager's retirement plan and creating a backup fund.

Handle your resources wisely (assistance is less costly than replacement), but above all, take care of your health.

1. State Your Life Objectives

What does freedom from the rat race mean to you? Everyone wants it, but that's too nebulous an aim. What you actually want to do is be clear about amounts and deadlines. The more specific your goals are, the more likely it is that you'll achieve them.

Note these three objectives:

1) The expectations of your way of life;

2) The amount that should be in your ledger in order for that to be possible; and

3) At what age is it too late to save that amount?

After that, count backwards from your cutoff time age to your ongoing age, placing financial mileposts at regular intervals between the two dates. Carefully record all amounts and cutoff periods, and place the objective page in front of your financial fastener.

2. Establish a Spending Plan Each Month

The best approach to make sure that all expenses are paid and reserve monies are allocated appropriately is to create and follow a monthly family financial plan. Regular routines also help you achieve your goals and strengthen your resolve when faced with the temptation to indulge a bit too much.

3. Completely handle your credit cards

While understudy loans, contracts, and similar advances typically have a lot lower financing costs, taking care of them isn't a crisis; paying these lower-interest credits on time is still important because timely payments will build a respectable credit score, Visas and other high-interest consumer advances are detrimental to establishing long-term financial stability. Make it a highlight to take care of the full balance each month.

4. Establish Autonomous Savings

Pay yourself first. Enrol in your manager's retirement plan and fully utilise any matching commitment benefit—basically, free money. It's also wise to have a scheduled commitment to a money market fund or something similar and a scheduled withdrawal into a backup fund that can be used for unforeseen expenses.

Ideally, the money for the retirement asset and the covert stash should be taken out of your record on the day you receive your cheque so it never comes into your possession.

Keep in mind that the recommended amount to save in a secret stash depends on your specific circumstances. Moreover, tax-advantaged retirement accounts come with terms that make it difficult to access your money should you suddenly need it, so that record shouldn't be your primary backup stash.

5. Get Investing Right Away

Bear markets, which are terrible stock exchanges, can lead people to doubt the wisdom of financial planning, but overall, there's never been a better way to grow your money. The allure of self-multiplying dividends will grow your money significantly, but it does take a long time to achieve meaningful growth.

Nevertheless, keep in mind that, for everyone save for knowledgeable investors, it would be a mistake to attempt the kind of stock selection made famous by moguls like Warren Buffett. Open an online money market fund that makes it easy for you to figure out how to contribute, create a reasonable portfolio, and make weekly or monthly commitments to it organically. We've positioned the best online agents for beginners to help you get started.

It can be difficult to achieve freedom from the rat race even in the face of growing responsibilities, financial difficulties, health problems, and excessive spending. Still, it is possible with careful planning and discipline.

SPEAK WITH YOUR DEBTORS

Once you have sorted out your financial facts, you must speak with your creditors to acquire their support for whatever the purpose of your visit or appointment was. This merely serves to confirm that the earlier actions are vital since they give you the information you need to get ready to meet with your creditors.

These kinds of visits are typically made in an attempt to persuade the creditors to extend the due date for payments before taking action to collect the outstanding balance, which is typically determined by the collateral submitted with the loan request. Due to their incapacity to make mortgage payments, some people have their homes foreclosed upon, and in other situations, banks or loan sharks may seize your possessions, including your car or household appliances.

It is necessary to have your financial information and knowledge of their policies readily available when visiting your credit report. As a result, this will be crucial in having your status reviewed and giving you another chance. It is also crucial that you arrange a visit before they start their house visits so you can assess what they will auction or possibly repossess in order to get the loan. This will demonstrate your dedication to their work and your cooperation. This will enable you to make an impression on them and gain their support.

Bring up the methods and steps you are taking to ensure that you solve the debt problem that you have with them, and that is when you present your budget, which incorporates the repayment of the loan. The meeting will allow you to explain the reasons and factors that have contributed to your failure to fulfil your part of the agreement, which was to repay the loan amount by the end of the stipulated and agreed period. You can even present the necessary evidence, which could be your income statement and other necessary documents. It will be equally necessary at that point to specify the length of the extension you intend to take in order to make the loan's complete payment.

Being joined by your financial advisor would be beneficial as well, as they can serve as a source of support for you during the presentation and assist you in clarifying any topics that the creditors might not understand.

Given the points in your presentation that influence your repayment plan, you might be able to persuade them to reduce your interest rates in certain circumstances. They might lower the rate to a manageable level so that you labour less and have less strain.

Consolidating Your Debt in Chapter Nine This is the procedure for submitting a new loan application, but this time, it will be used to pay off your current debt balance. This method is regarded as highly beneficial as it facilitates a quicker and easier loan repayment process. It also frees your mind from a lot of other bills that you will eventually pay off, so you can concentrate on paying off this one big sum.

The primary advantage of the consolidation option is that it enables you to receive reduced interest rates on your loans, making it possible for you to make monthly loan repayments and still have money left over for consumption.

Since it keeps goods from being repossessed and provides you more time to reassess your financial position, consolidating debt is typically a simpler solution. However, it's crucial that you carefully read the terms and circumstances before taking the easy route, even if it means digging yourself into a potentially deeper hole this time.

Make sure you are aware of the amount you will receive, the time you have to pay it back, and the total amount you will have to pay when the allotted time has passed. who should assist you in selecting the best choices.

Additionally, you want to research interest rates and compare those offered by several institutions. To avoid falling for scams like many others, you ought to be able to select the greatest loan servicer. Make sure you appreciate the specifics of interest rates and whether or not they are likely to change. If they are, make sure you also understand the potential causes of this change, whether they are favourable or unfavourable. However, in this instance, the hope will be focused more on the interest rates declining at that point for the benefit of the loaned individual.

However, the debt consolidation procedure assists a person in paying off their outstanding obligations. It prevents them from falling behind on their payments, which would otherwise result in a negative credit report.

SAVINGS AND INVESTMENTS CHAPTER TEN

Obviously, no one is thinking about this while they pay off their bills and view this financial advice as going in the wrong direction. Financial advisors typically advise their clients to save even if they are in debt since it will still have a good financial impact, even though most individuals believe that saving should only be done when they are in a secure financial state.

You should start saving as soon as possible because financial assistance may be necessary for unanticipated and unpleasant events that arise in life. Saving is difficult because we are sometimes too busy taking care of our immediate needs and activities to think about long-term planning.

When you pay off your obligations completely, your savings from while you were in debt will protect you from needing to borrow money again. Savings are intended to protect you from any difficult economic periods you may experience while building the highly desired, financially secure portfolio.

Rainy days are a great time to have savings since they save you from having to seek cash, which may be embarrassing. Another advantage is that savings earn income, but much more slowly and insignificantly than interest from debt. As a result, you are able to get in more money than you had saved.

Investing is similar to saving money, except that the goal is to increase your investment. However, things might change, and the shares you purchase may decline, leading to negative indexes and a potential loss on your investment.

The risk associated with company investing typically calls for financial know-how. This is the reason why financial counsellors recommend investing in things like healthcare, cars, education for one's future children, and even death. Funds for education will guarantee that your kids attend school worry-free and receive quality medical care.

Therefore, savings and investments protect your future and spare you the trouble of applying for loans and requesting money from other sources.

Without Bill Gates' invention of Microsoft Windows, things would have most likely changed drastically. But because of his creativity, he has not only improved everyone's life on the planet but has also attained the maximum level of financial independence.

While perseverance pays off in the long run, creativity and ingenuity are equally valuable. Many people put in a lot of effort, yet the types of occupations they do never allow them to become financially independent. Rather, they will continue to increase the wealth of the world's millionaires and billionaires.

Remember that the journey to financial achievement starts in your head before you take any further action. You are not going anywhere if you do not believe in yourself. You have to understand the value of self-motivation towards prosperity and the power of your mind.

You should think about doing a few things to cultivate the proper mindset for financial success. will shape the methods you use to manage your assets and finances like a wealthy person.

Observing those around you ought to be among your initial priorities. They have such a strong impact on your thinking that it will affect how you go about creating money for yourself, whether they be friends, coworkers, or even family.

Like fingerprints, the people in your immediate vicinity are all different. They all have different ways of thinking about and earning money. Therefore, you shouldn't always follow their lead. Though you should always keep in mind that you are the one with the last say in your life, counsel has no negative value.

You should avoid hanging around with folks who are overly focused on their careers and insufficiently imaginative. Whether they are your closest friends or family members doesn't matter; if they have a particular method of thinking about making money, make sure it works for you.

Generally speaking, what is one man's treasure is another man's garbage. When attempting to get wealthy, it might make a huge distinction if you are able to locate a legitimate reason when most people are unable to. The only way to cultivate a successful mindset is to avoid the demoralising aspects of friends who hold different opinions from your own.

Everyone close to you should be very cautious since you can quickly become influenced by their ideas and viewpoints. One of the most important relationship lessons is that the people you surround yourself with reflect everything about you. This idea also relates to the pursuit of financial security.

Spending time with creative individuals will shape who you become, so if you surround yourself with them often, you'll find that your creativity eventually blossoms. You can, therefore, generate significant business concepts that will make you stand out from the competition.

Developing the proper mentality requires you to examine your thoughts on the world's affluent individuals in addition to those who are in your immediate vicinity. You probably believe that because of their wealth, billionaires and other wealthy people you have come into contact with are unethical or even evil.

But if you want to cultivate the proper mindset, you shouldn't hold onto any jealousy. Being jealous is a weak emotion that will keep you stuck in debt and restrict your vision. Recall that, like you, the majority of affluent people most likely started from nothing. Discard beliefs like "money does not grow on trees" and "if I become wealthy, there won't be enough for everyone else." Most people who have studied economics and other money-related courses believe that they will instantly become wealthy, but the financial system is not as simple as you might imagine.

Recall that despite failing out of college, Bill Gates has more fortune than some of the world's smartest individuals. How was this accomplished? Through adopting the appropriate mentality. Since your life is your own, you should reevaluate what you believe to be true about wealthy individuals.

If you have aspirations of being wealthy, follow through on them and avoid connecting bad things in your life with the quality of life that affluent individuals have attained. Develop the mindset of affluent individuals by having faith in your capacity to achieve financial success.

Have a future-focused perspective if you want to cultivate the proper mindset for financial success. If you can't see yourself in a few days, a few months, or even years from now, it's hard to suddenly find yourself wealthy. You have a direction when your vision is clear. If you want to succeed financially, decide what kind of lifestyle you want to lead and what kind of labour you want to perform to get there. It is important to consider the direction you want your life to go since it will spur you on to take action.

Financial success cannot be attained by only imitating the actions of others or obsessing over trying to become just like them. Allow affluent individuals to serve as role models for you, but design your own life and your vision for your immediate and long-term goals.

Create an attitude of financial success by considering how you can generate passive income. You should consider strategies to earn money other than the conventional methods you are accustomed to, much like chess players who can locate competitions that offer them real prize money.

Keep in mind that while work can help you get where you want to go, it is not the end all be all. You will accelerate your path to financial success if you can combine your work with a passive source of income. You can harness passive income to achieve financial security.

Setting Financial Targets

One of the most important steps on your path to financial security is setting financial goals. Here's how to accomplish it:

1. Consider Your Ambitions: Consider carefully what you hope to accomplish with your money. Think about your long- and short-term goals. Consider the following: ● What are my top priorities when it comes to money? ● Where do I see myself in five, ten, or twenty years? ● What would bring me contentment and security in terms of money?

2. Sort Your Objectives: To help you prioritise and keep your financial goals organised, divide them into distinct categories. Typical categories consist of:

Short-Term Objectives: These can include buying a new automobile, saving for a trip, or paying off credit card debt. They are usually reachable in the next one to two years.

Intermediate-Term Objectives: These cover a period of three to five years and may include beginning a business or saving for a down payment on a house.

Long-Term Goals: These are your overarching plans, including preparing for retirement, putting money down for your kids' college tuition, or leaving a legacy.

3. Designate Particulars and Numbers: Set quantifiable and precise goals for yourself. Give specifics on how much and by when you want to save, rather than just declaring, "I want to save for retirement." For instance, by the time I'm 65, I want $1 million in my retirement account.

Prioritise Your Objectives: Identify the objectives that are most significant to you and your family. Setting priorities enables you to devote your time and resources appropriately. Think about things like influence, urgency, and personal values.

5. Take Timeframes Into Account: Recognise that every goal has a different deadline. While long-term goals benefit from persistent, long-range planning, short-term goals could need more urgent attention.

6. Take Life Stages Into Account: Be aware that as you move through different life stages, your financial objectives may also change. Your 20s

goals could not be the same as your 40s or 60s goals.

7. Consistently review and update: Your financial objectives are subject to change. Your goals may need to be adjusted over time as your circumstances change in life. Review your goals often and make any adjustments.

8. Set SMART objectives: Put the SMART acronym (Specific, Measurable, Achievable, Relevant, and Time-bound) to work for your objectives. Your goals become more achievable and actionable using this approach.

9. Seek Professional Advice: To get advice tailored to your specific situation, talk to a financial advisor if you're

unclear on how to prioritise or set your financial goals.

You can create a financial plan to help you reach your financial objectives after you've determined which ones are most important. Setting and maintaining clear goals enables you to make well-informed financial decisions that support your goals.

www.ingramcontent.com/pod-product-compliance
Lightning Source LLC
Chambersburg PA
CBHW071643210326
41597CB00017B/2096